CLASSICAL MODERN ART
COLORING BOOK

Volume 6
Classic Art Coloring Book Series

Drawings and text by Denise McGill

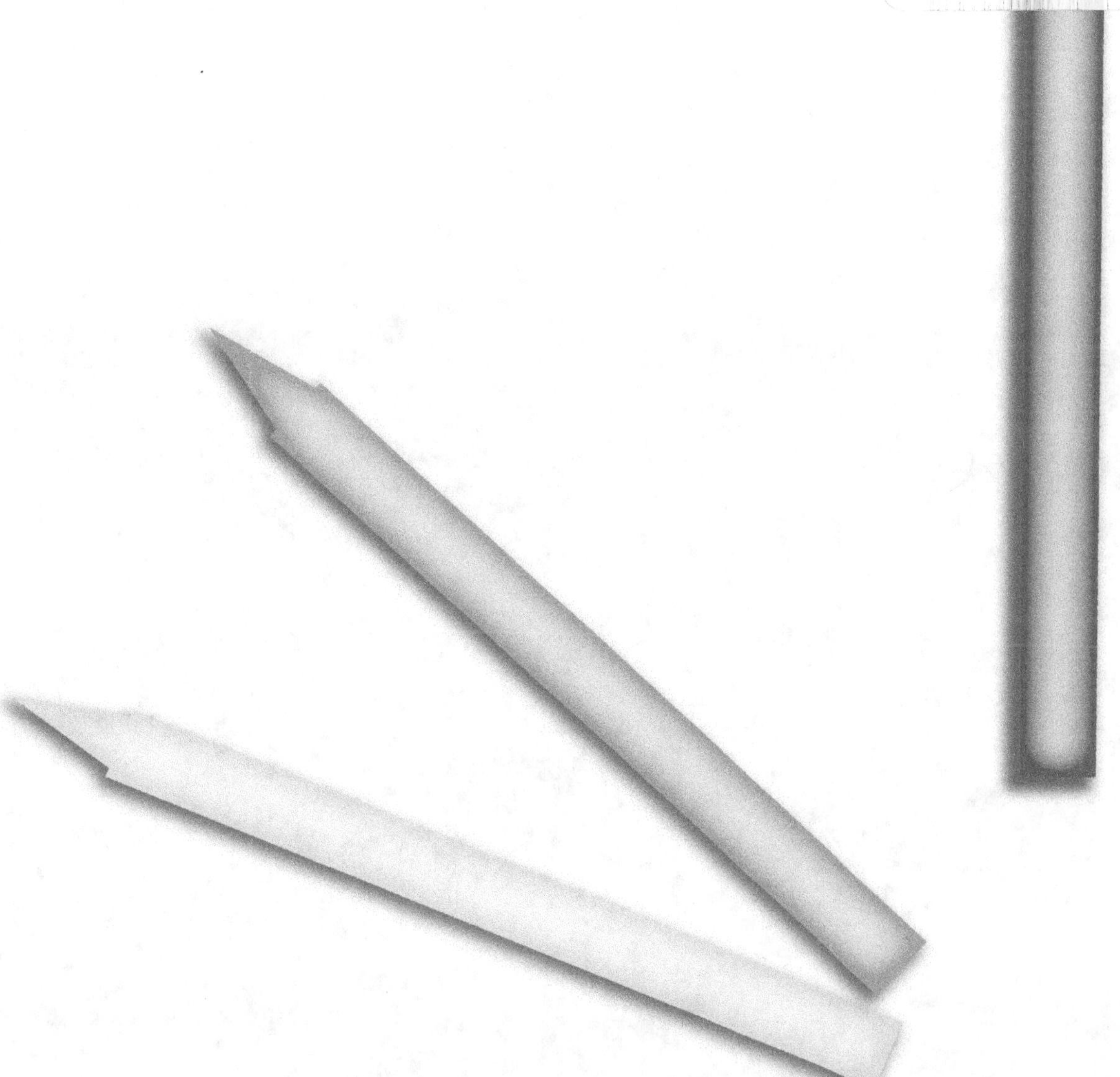

classical modern art
COLORING BOOK

Table of Contents

COLORING PAGES

As simplistic as it may seem, coloring the art of a renowned artist is an excellent method of introducing art to students. They see the work and recognize it. They may not be able to name the artist and year just by having colored the piece, but they will always remember it. To add more to the learning experience, it is suggested that you check out a library book on each artist or go online and look up the work of art after allowing the children to color it their way. Then seeing how the artist painted the piece, what colors were used how large or small the finished piece was, helps enforce the learning experience. It is up to each educator to decide on whether to check out the art before the students color the page or after. If they see the piece before they color theirs, they may be influence to copy, or use the same colors the artist did. If they see the piece after, they may be surprised at the color choice of the artist and even pleased with their own choices.

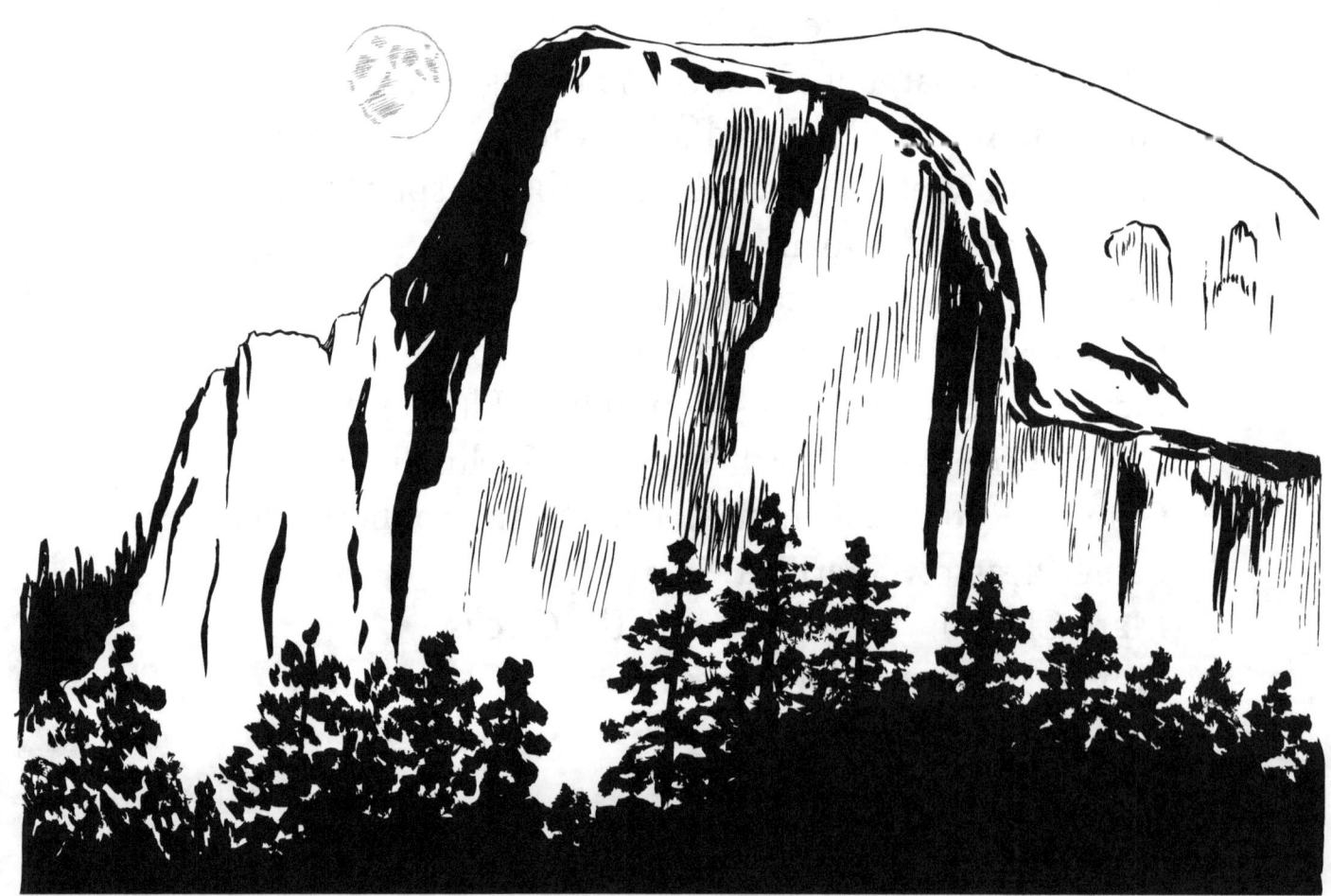

after the Impressionists

1880-1900 Impressionists

The Impressionists changed everything about how we see the world. They were more concerned with light and color than capturing the perfect form. It is almost what you see when you squint your eyes on a sunny day. Many believe that Renoir and Monet had vision problems that were not corrected because of the soft, out-of-focus paintings they produced. Whether this is true or not, it changed the direction of art forever. After the Impressionists, artists were free to experiment with light, color, form and emotion, which lead into the Modern Era Art.

Following the Impressionists were the Post-Impressionists, taking the art a bit further in the loose treatment of light and color. Later the Ex-pressionists and on into the Modern Art era.

From here there were a dizzing number of art movements some only lasting a few years to a decade. Since there are too many to name, I will touch on only a few of the most notable.

1885-1920 Post-Impressionists

The Post-Impressionists weren't an art movement as much as a group of artists who took Impressionism a step further. Notably they were Gauguin, Van Gogh, Seurat, Cezanne, and a few others. They took the capturing of light and color of the Impressionists and added a return to line and form. To me they took the softness and out-of-focus look of the Impressionist and added longer strokes with the brushes so that the pure colors were more visible in some cases. In other cases they used dots of pure color arranged so the eye of the audience did the blending.

1890-1939   Fauves and Expressionists

The Fauves (which means "wild beasts" in French), mostly lead by Matisse and Rouault, were so called because of their hard lines and bold colors. They used pure color and bold placement of lines and shapes to express and emotion or feeling. They way they painted affected other movements of art to follow.

1905-1939   Cubism and Futurism

Picasso and Braque, in France, invented cubism by taking form and reducing it to its basic geometric shapes, circles, squares, triangles. This is the way most artists explain form and shape, but Picasso and Braque took it a step further by leaving these block shapes in the painting.

In Italy, futurism was born of a desire to take art into the industrial age, portraying factories and industry and embracing machines.

1922-1939   Surrealism

Surrealism is about uncovering the hidden meanings in the mind and subconscious. At this time Freud had published his writings on psychoanalysis and the working of the mind became foremost in the public conscious. Dali is considered the quintessential Surrealist, depicting the subconscious in a way that still causes people to pause and think.

1945-Present   Abstract Expressionism

With the outbreak of war (World War II 1939-1945) most movements in art were interrupted and just surviving because the utmost goal. After the war a return to normalcy was not as easy as it would seam. Most countries had to pick up the pieces and money for art was scarce. What came out of the chaos was a form of art that threw out all the rules and recognizable form, keeping only self-expression as the goal. Color was to portray life and emotion, the inner-most spark of life and feeling, raw emotion.

Late 1950s-Present   Pop and Op art

The Pop Art movement came out of a revolt against Abstract Expressionism, and an embrace of the mundane and ordinary, like soup cans. Warhol was a leader in this movement, finding lasting beauty in the ordinary. It was fun and readily accepted. Op Art came from a shortening of the term optical illusion and was in sync with the psychedelic times of the 60s.

1970s-Present

Performance art, conceptual art, digital art, shock art, to name a few, have been some of the movements in the 30-40 years to present. Art is changing at lightening speed in keeping with the digital age. As we move more toward a global community where we are all connected, there will be fewer isolated movements and more art that spans the globe. Art has a connective quality, needing no language to interpret it. It is appreciated or not on its own merits. This makes art an international language, perfect for the global age.

eDVaRD MUNCH, 1863-1944

The Scream, 1893

Oil on canvas

Munch was a Norwegian painter in the Expressionist style. He focused on psychological themes and influenced many other artistic movements. The Scream is so iconic that along with the Mona Lisa, by Da Vinci, and American Gothic, by Grant Wood, it is known wherever it is seen. Munch suffered many tragedies in his life, from the tragic death of his sister to tuberculosis, and his father's death and a brother, destruction of several paintings in a fire, and more. He allowed his paintings to help him get out the pain and stress of loss. Many of his cotemporaries didn't understand and eventually he had a nervous breakdown due to drinking and depression.

The Scream is of an agonizing figure against a blood red sky; the landscape of Oslofjord, viewed from the hill of Ekeberg, in Oslo, Norway.

THE SCREAM

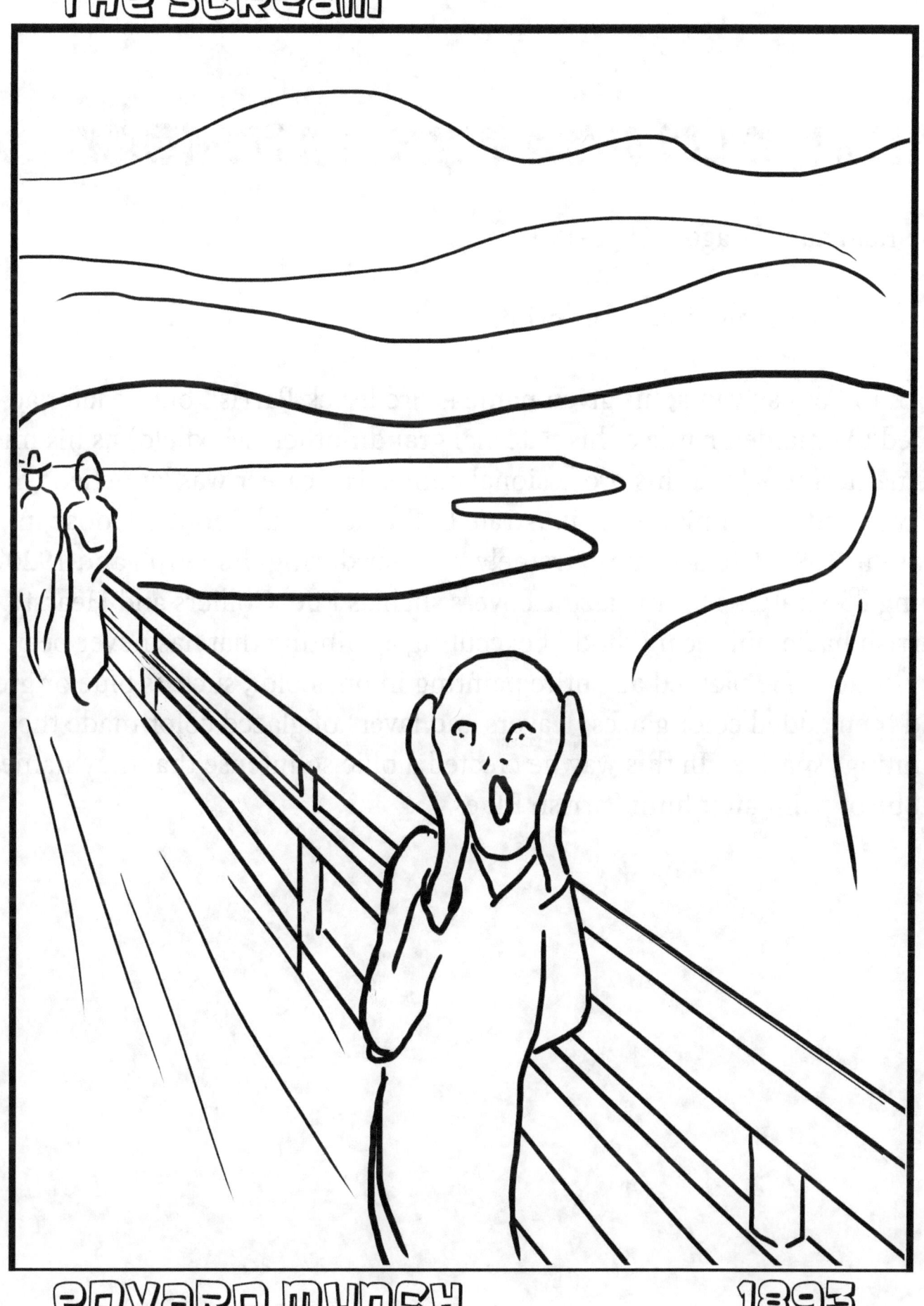

EDVARD MUNCH   1893

MAXFIELD PARRISH, 1870-1966

The Reluctant Dragon, 1900-1901

Oil on Canvas, reproduced as prints

Born in Pennsylvania, his given name is Frederick Parrish but he later adopted the maiden name of his paternal grandmother (Maxfield) as his middle name and later as his professional name. His career was launched when he received a commission to illustrate L. Frank Baum's Mother Goose in Prose in 1897. He became extremely popular during the 1910's and 1920's doing illustrations for magazine covers such as Life, Colliers and Hearst's. Parrish had a unique method of executing a painting that has never been duplicated. He painted an entire painting in one color, such as blue or grey, and then added color glazes. Layers and layers of glazed color made the paintings sparkle. In this way he created a blue so intense that they named a tube of paint after him: Parrish Blue.

THE RELUCTANT DRAGON

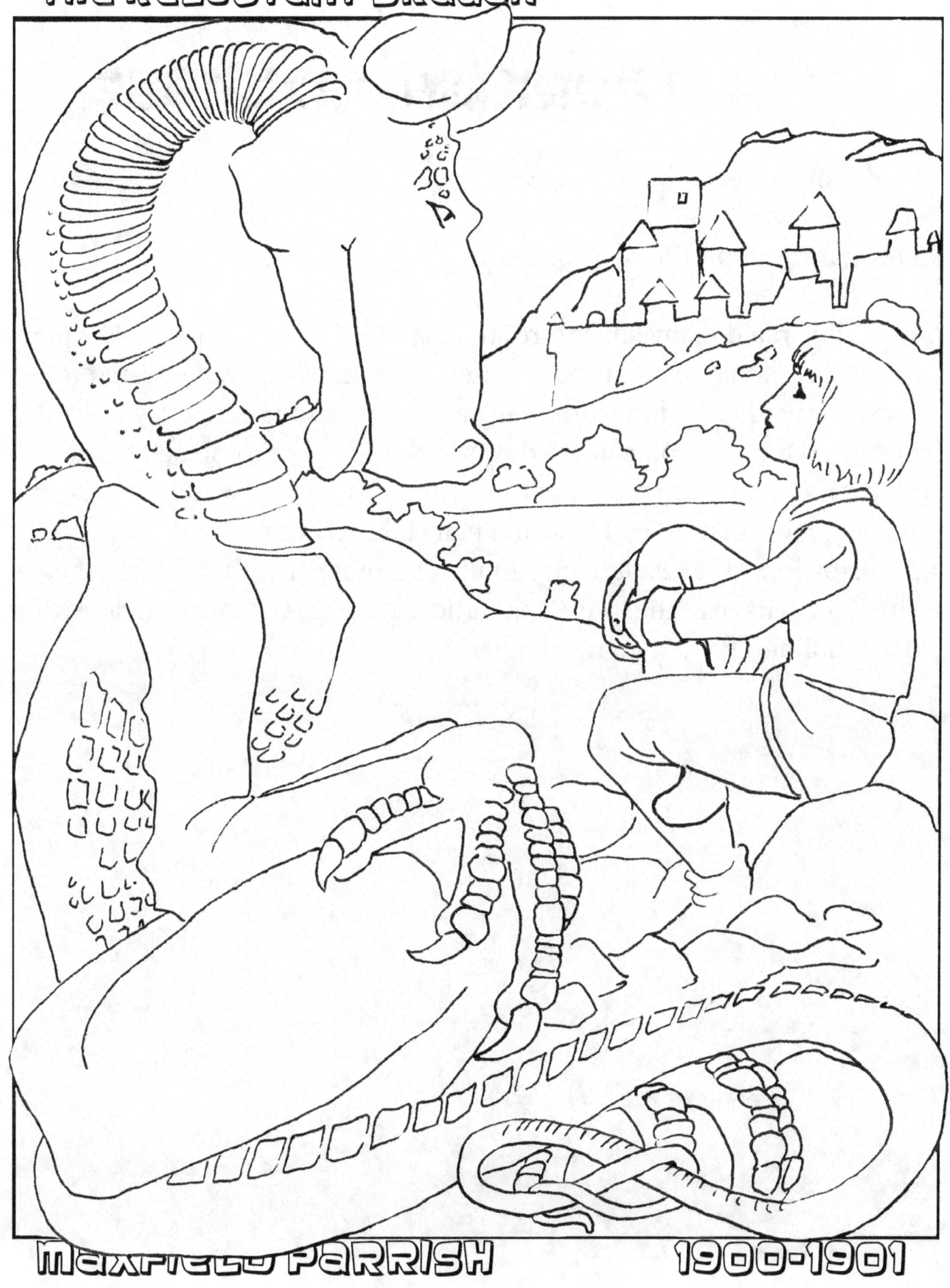

MAXFIELD PARRISH   1900-1901

maxfield parrish, 1870-1966

Sinbad Plots Against the Giant, 1906

Oil on Canvas, reproduced as prints

Parrish illustrated many adventure stories published in America. His posters and calendar art are still sought after. Norman Rockwell referred to Parish as "my idol" and in truth many artists have sought to copy his brilliant style. One technique he used was to drape a geometric patterned cloth over a figure so that the pattern (usually black and white squares or polka dots) was distorted. He would painstakingly draw from the photo each distortion. The result being, an illusion of form without the bother of shadows. His paintings were romanticized images of the magical world and a childhood fantasy come to life.

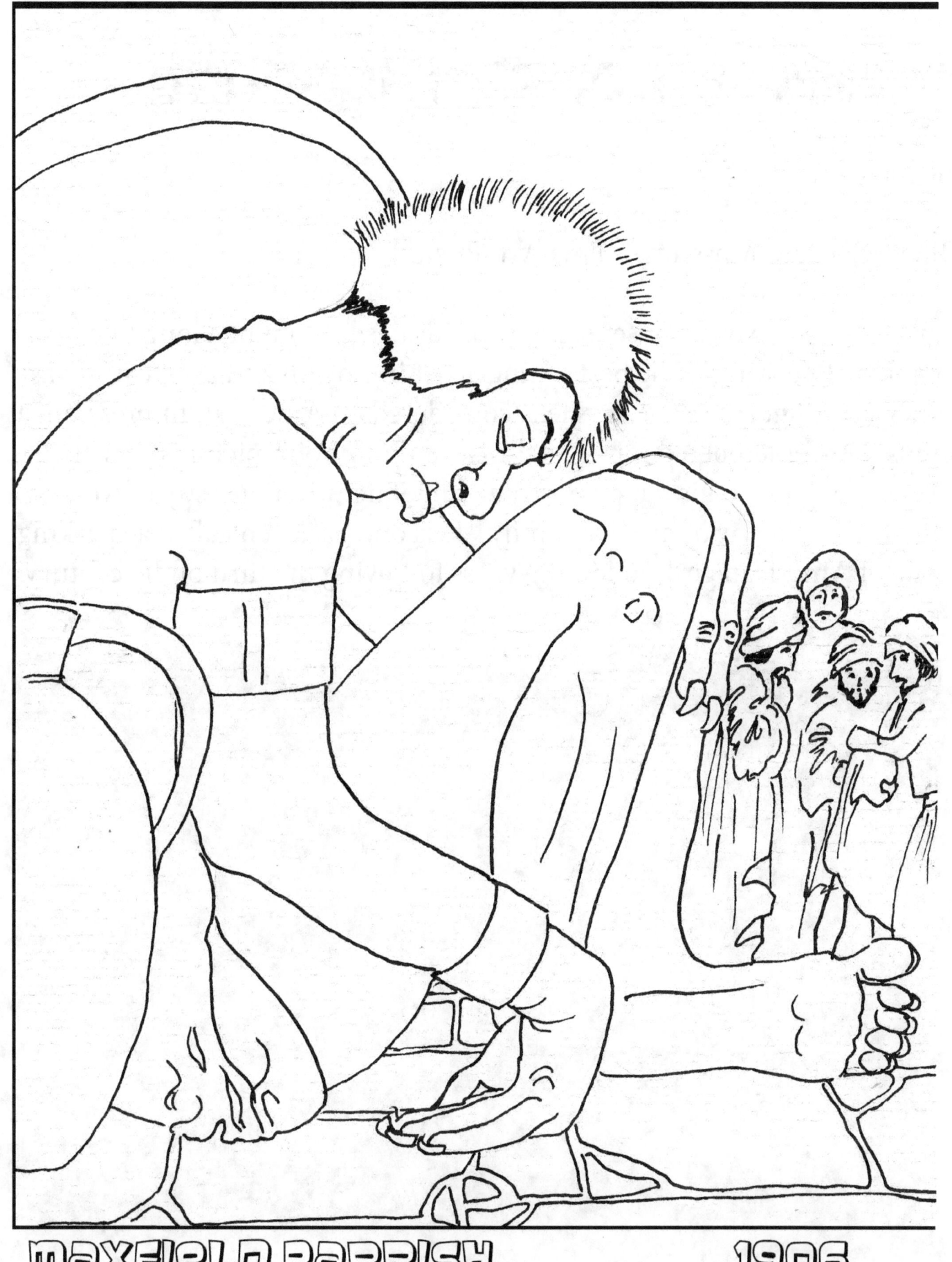

Maxfield Parrish 1906

Frank W. Benson, 1862-1951

Eleanor, 1907

Oil on Canvas, Museum of Fine Art, Boston

Born in Salem, Massachusetts, Benson was descendant of a long line of sea captains. Benson was the best selling artist in Boston and even earned as much as six figures in a year. He is considered an American Impressionist and is best remembered for his etchings and dry point pictures, mostly of birds in flight. But his happy portraits full of light were mostly of women and girls and many of his own family. This one has been called a sparking scene of American girlhood in the years following the turn of the century.

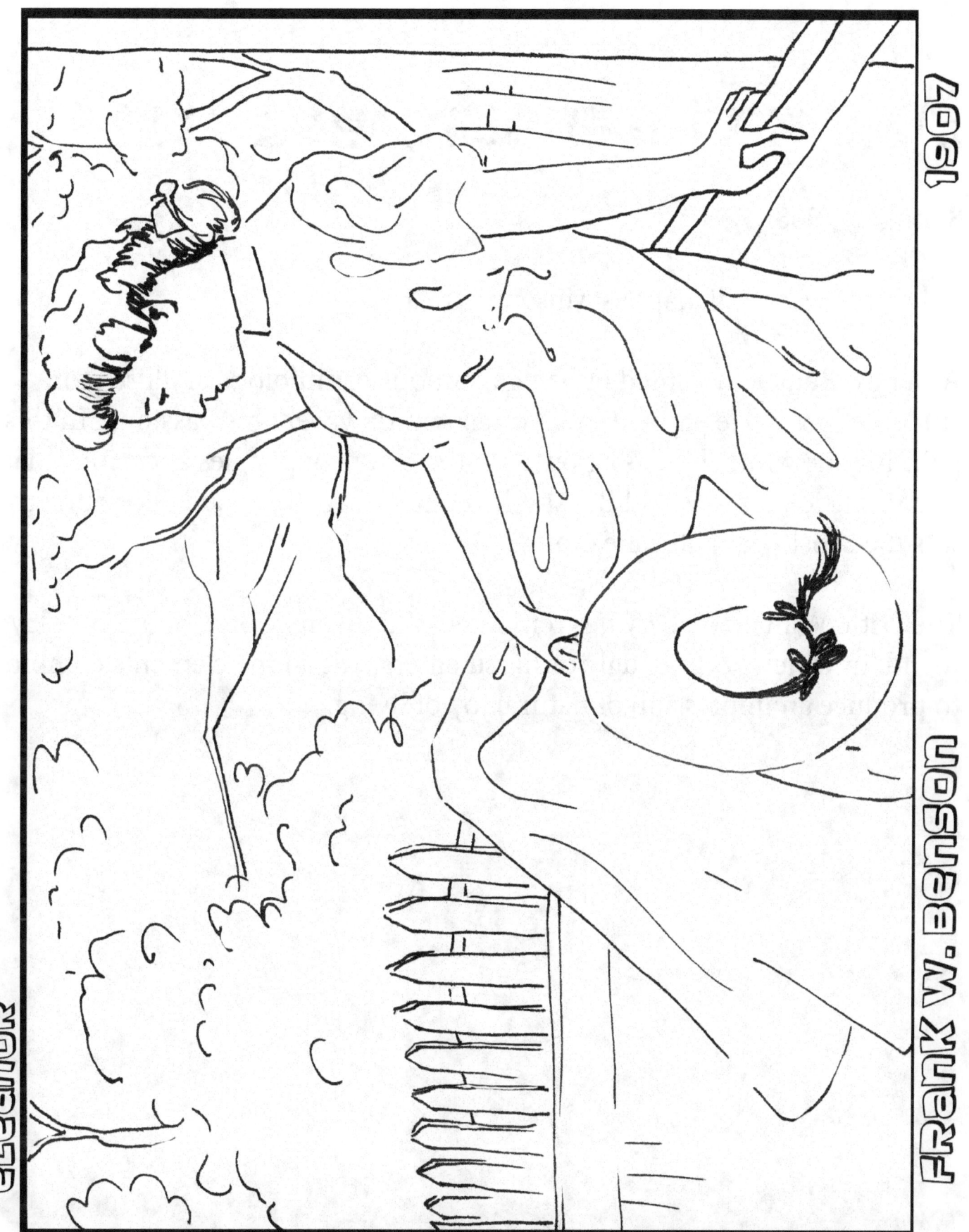

eLeanoR

FRanK W. Benson   1907

FRanK W. Benson, 1862-1951

Sunlight, 1908

Oil on Canvas, Indianapolis Museum of Art

As a boy, Benson dreamed of being a famous ornithological illustrator, studying birds. He painted them often and they were his passion. In this painting the white dress is aglow with the colors of purples and pinks that add to the idealized world Benson loved painting. The model for Sunlight was the artist's daughter Eleanor.

The critic William H. Downes remarked of Benson's work, "It is a holiday world, in which nothing ugly or harsh enters, but all the elements combine to produce an impression of natural joy of living."

SUNLIGHT

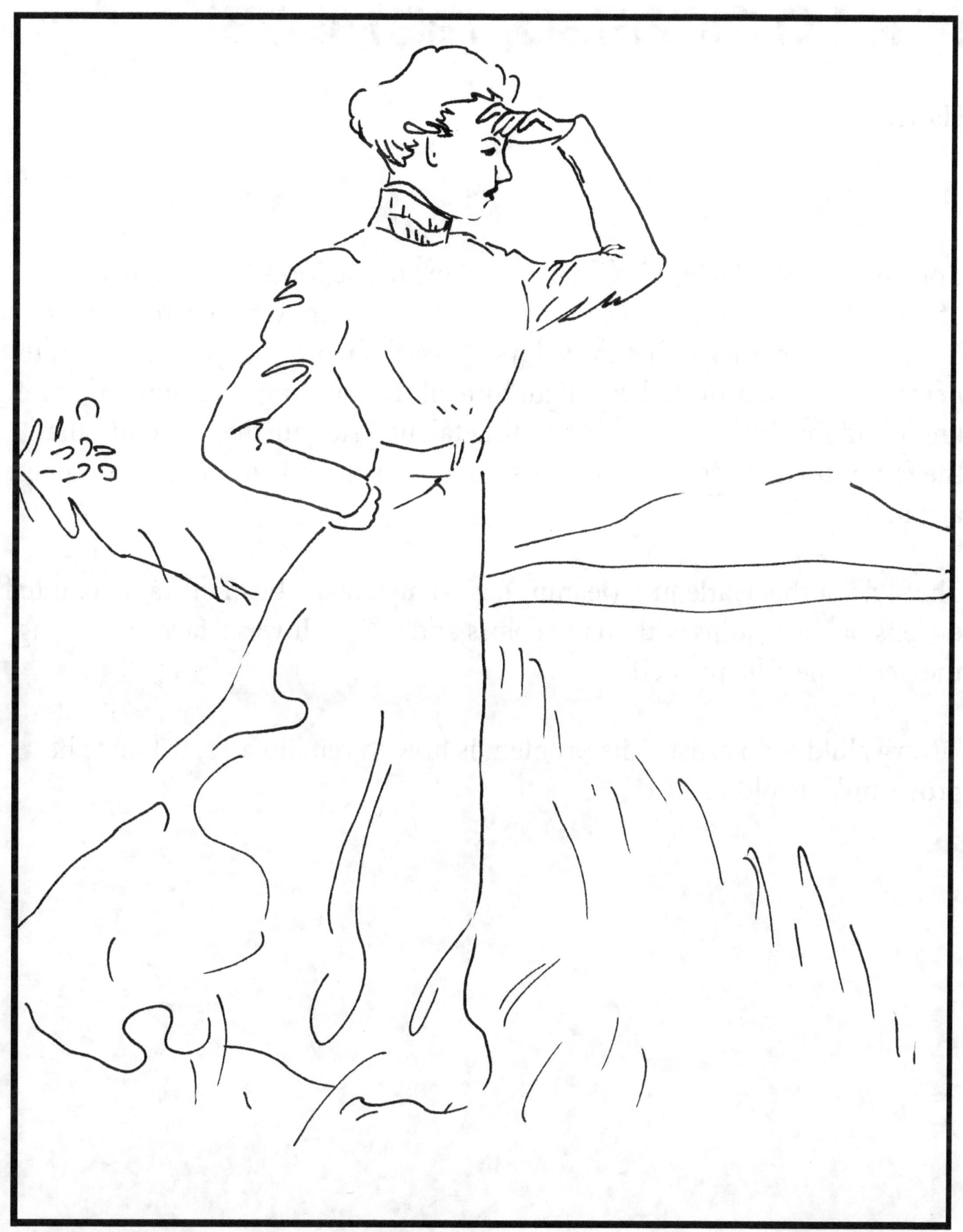

FRANK W. BENSON   1908

PABLO PICASSO, 1881-1973

Harlequin, 1909

Oil on Canvas,

Born in Malaga, Spain, Picasso became one of the most influential artists of the 20th century. Famous for developing Cubism, very few people did not know his name. In his early days Picasso's favorite subjects were circus performers. After his father taught him all the painting techniques that he knew and saw his son take his painting talent a step further, it is said that the father turned over his paintbrushes to his son and vowed never to paint again.

The style of this Harlequin (leaning), is Analytical Cubism. Picasso painted dozens of Harlequins with many colors and styles. It was a favorite among the performers he painted

"Every child is an artist. The problem is how to remain an artist once he grows up." Pablo Picasso.

HARLEQUIN

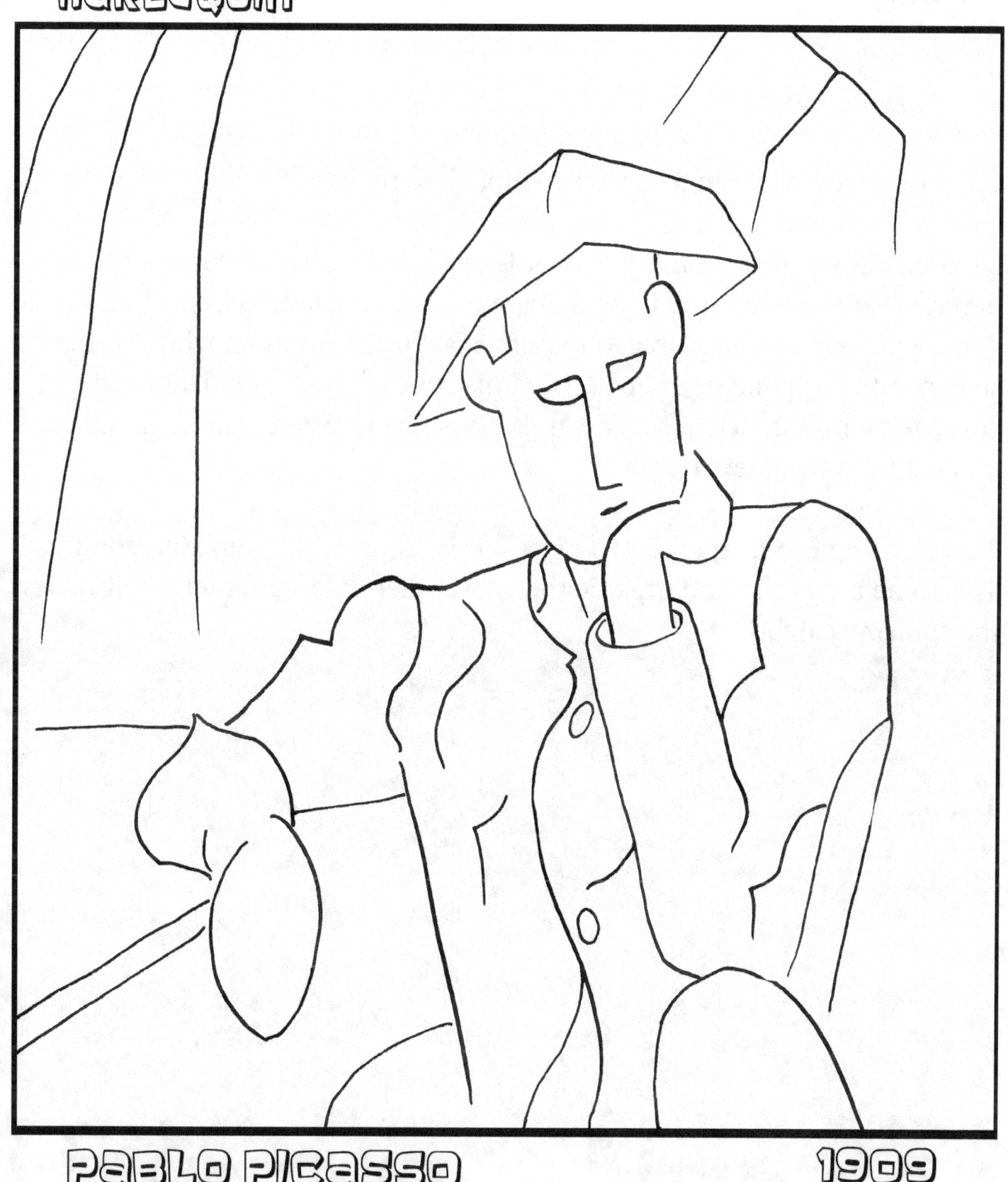

PABLO PICASSO   1909

JOHN SINGER SARGENT, 1856-1925

Two Girls Fishing, 1912

Oil on Canvas, Cincinnati Art Museum, Cincinnati Ohio

Sargent was an American Impressionist, born in Florence, Italy, but his parents were raised in the United States and he considered himself an American. He was encouraged to pursue art by his mother, who was herself an amateur painter. He patterned his style after Monet. He was discouraged with his lack of success in Paris, so he moved to London and made it his permanent home.

This painting is of Sargent's two nieces, Rose Marie and Reine Ormond. The scene is so calm and organic the viewer feels like he is there waiting for the squirmy catch.

TWO GIRLS FISHING

JOHN SINGER SARGENT

1912

noRman RockWeLL, 1894-1975

Grandfather with Two Children, December 24, 1921

Oil on Canvas

Norman Rockwell, an American painter and illustrator, found success early. By the age of 16 he was hired as the art director of Boys Life, the official magazine of Boy Scouts of America. When he was 21 he was doing freelance art for several magazines, when he walked into the editor's office at Saturday Evening Post with 2 paintings under his arm and got a job.

When he began doing the cover art for Saturday Evening Post and a few others, his fame was set. This was the 33rd cover Rockwell did for The Literary Digest.

"Without thinking too much about it in specific terms, I was showing the America I knew and observed to others who might not have noticed."
Norman Rockwell

GRANDFATHER WITH TWO CHILDREN

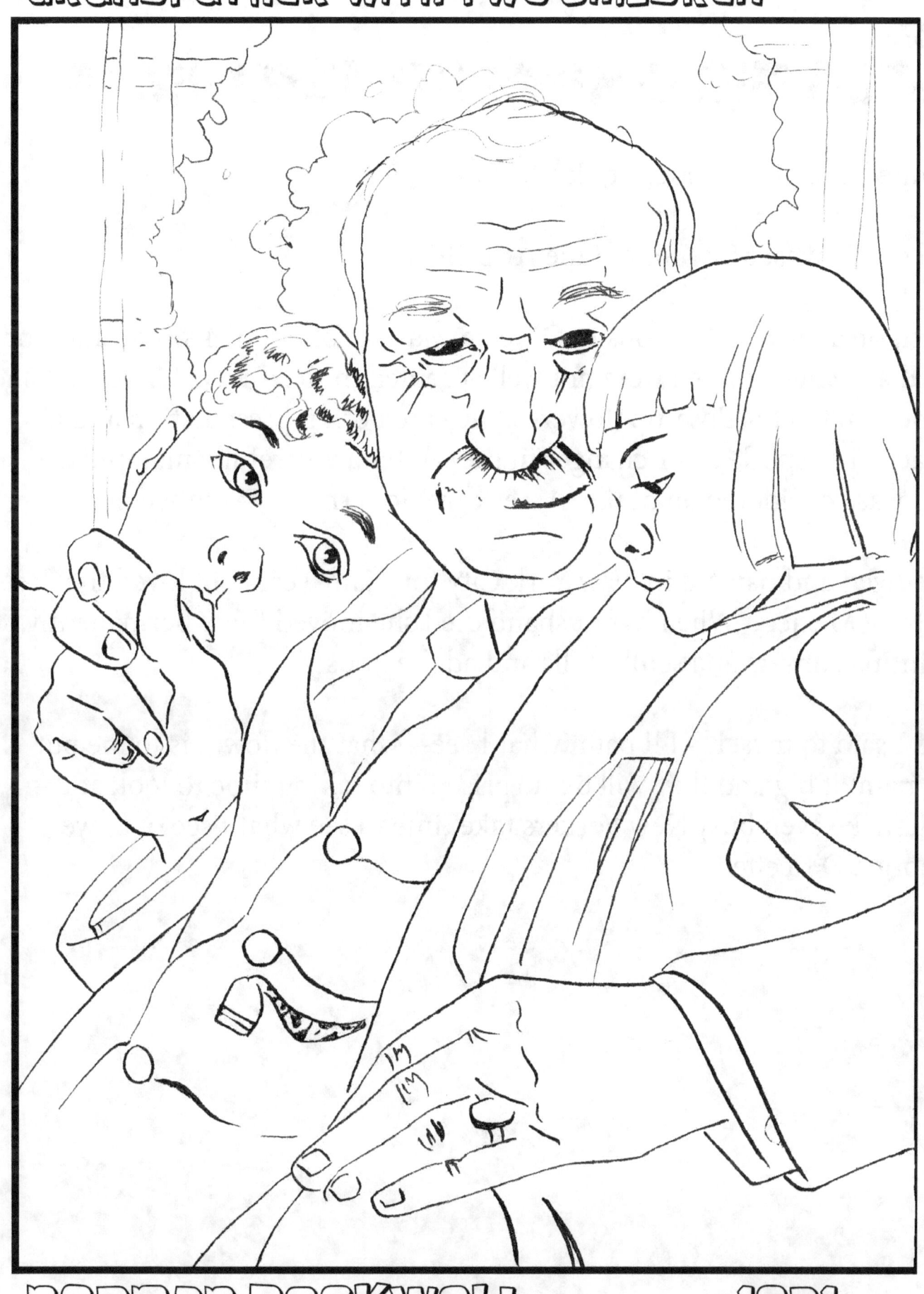

NORMAN ROCKWELL   1921

Georgia O'Keeffe, 1887-1986

White Rose With Larkspur No. 2, 1927

Oil on Canvas, Museum of Fine Arts, Boston

Born on a farm in Wisconsin, O'Keeffe was the oldest of 4 sisters and pursued art when women were not well accepted in the art world. At first she concentrated on close-up flowers. They are both representation and abstract. The subtle color changes in the whites are carefully manipulated. She was considered on of the American Modernism Art movement.

She lived and painted in New York City for many years but loved the desert of New Mexico. When her husband died she moved there permanently, painting sunsets and sculls, hills and adobe houses.

"So I said to myself—I'll paint what I see—what the flower is to me but I'll paint it big and they will be surprised into taking time to look at it—I will make even busy New Yorkers take time to see what I see of flowers."
Georgia O'Keeffe

WHITE ROSE WITH LARKSPUR NO 2

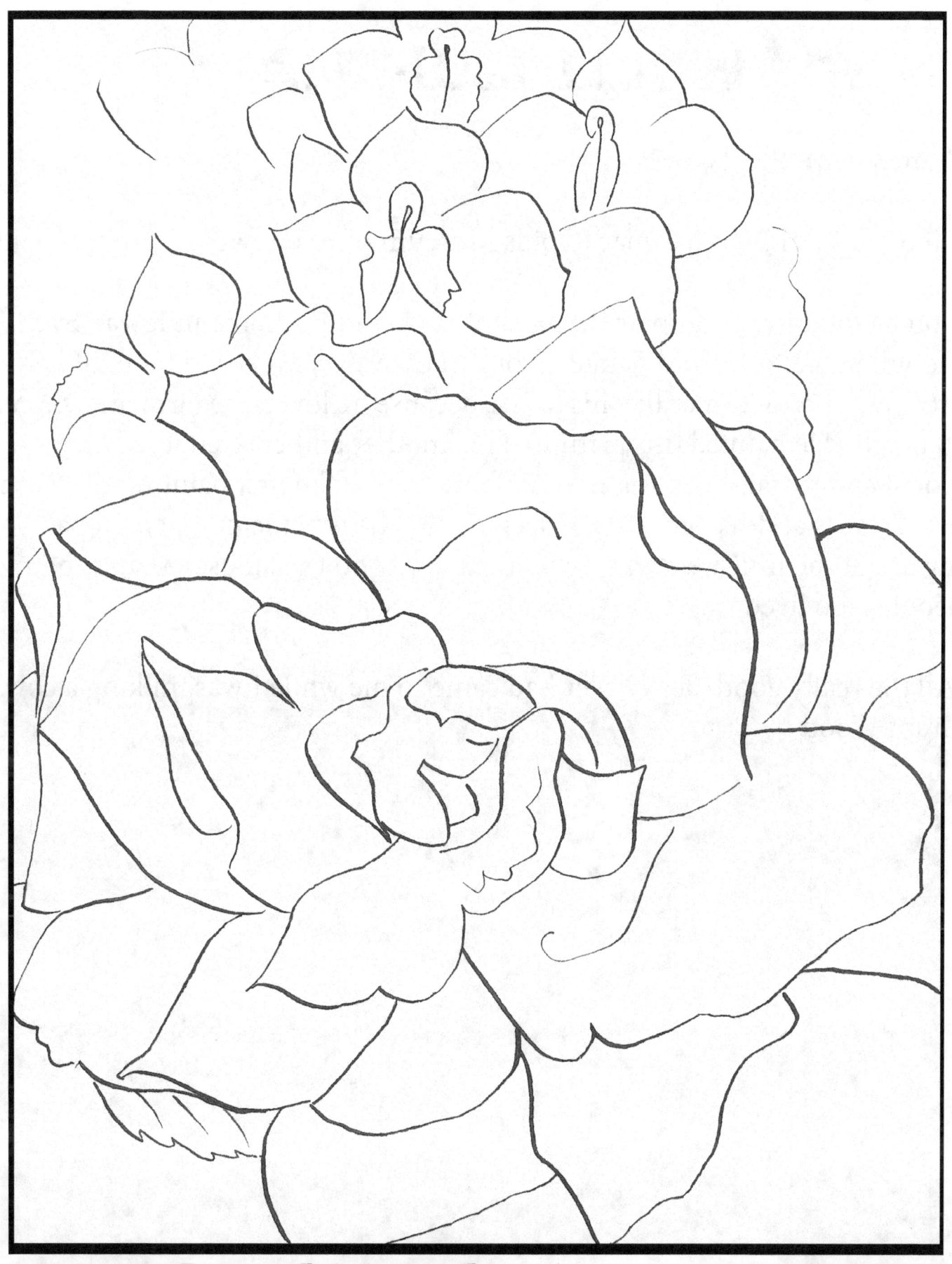

GEORGIA O'KEEFFE   1927

GRANT WOOD, 1891-1942

Woman with Plants, 1929

Oil on Upsom Board, Cedar Rapids Museum of Art, Iowa

Grant Wood lived and painted most of his life in his home in Iowa. Even though he sketched and painted from an early age, everyone thought he'd grow up to be a farmer like his father because he loved the farm and chores so much. He painted this picture of his mother and entered it in the regional county fair, winning Best of Show. It was the first painting that won him awards and recognition. It seemed that he was the first person painting about the mid-west who actually understood the landscape and the people who lived there.

"All the really good ideas I ever had came to me while I was milking a cow."
Grant Wood

WOMAN WITH PLANTS

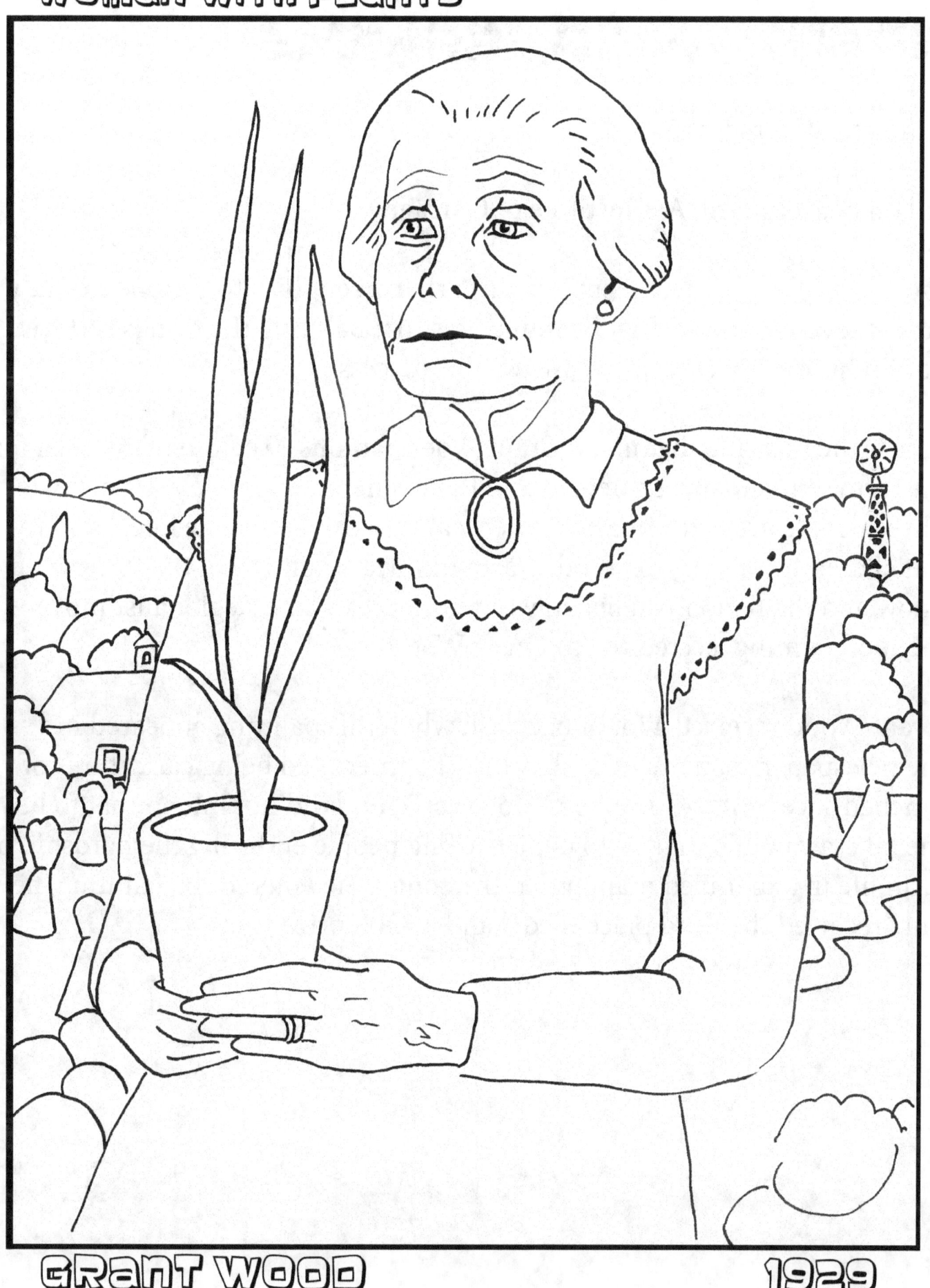

GRANT WOOD   1929

GRANT WOOD, 1891-1942

American Gothic, 1930

Oil on beaverboard, Art Institute of Chicago

Wood's mother wanted to support his art and sent him to Europe to study art for several years. What he found was that painting the things he loved best in his own backyard was the way to success.

This is the painting that made Grant Wood famous. The model he used for the farmer is actually his dentist and the woman who modeled is his sister. These people are patterned after the weatherworn people he knew and remembered from his years on the farm in Iowa. Painting of the things you know and the region you live in was referred to as the Regionalist movement of painting, accredited to Grant Wood.

Grant Wood received a lot of backlash when this painting appeared in the newspapers nationwide. They didn't appreciated being caricatures of pinched-faced Bible-thumpers. However Wood did not intend that to be the take-away. He wanted to depict strong people enduring the hardship of farm life in a dignified manner. In the contest he entered the painting, he only received the third place medal and a $300 prize.

american gothic

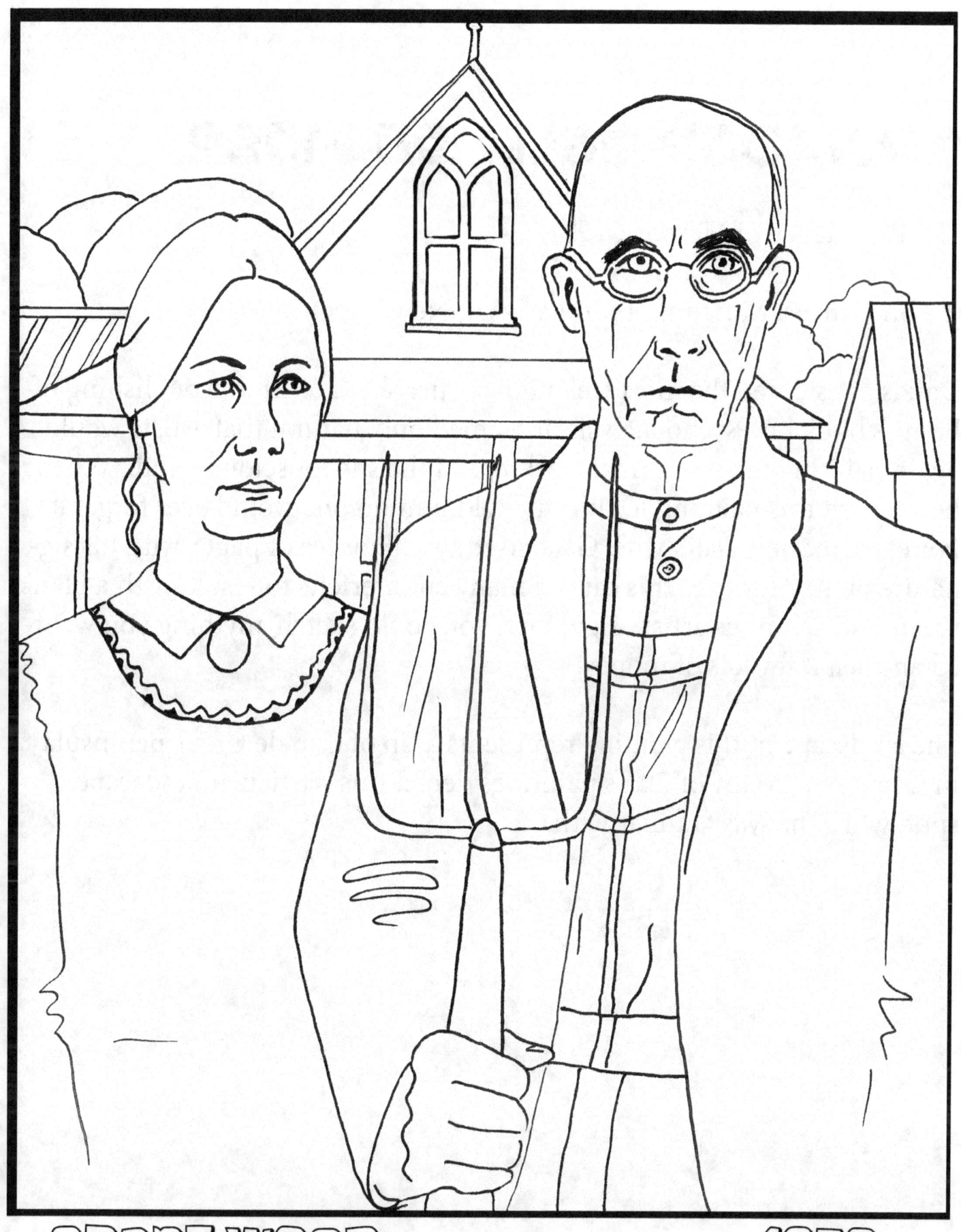

GRANT WOOD   1930

Salvador Dali, 1904-1989

The Persistence of Memory, 1931

Oil on Canvas, Museum of Modern Art, New York

Dali is considered the most well known surrealist. With the publishing of Freud's book on Psychoanalysis, it seemed only natural that artists would begin painting the subliminal workings of the subconscious mind. When he finished this painting, Dali's wife told him no one would ever forget it. For extra money, Dali's wife, Gala, used to sell pieces of paper with his signature on it. However this caused many counterfeits to result, with a blank paper and a famous artist's signature, you could sketch anything you wanted and sell it for lots of money.

The landscape in this painting represents a tip of Cap de Creus peninsula in Catalonia. Many of Dali's paintings depict this particular landscape spot, which he was familiar with.

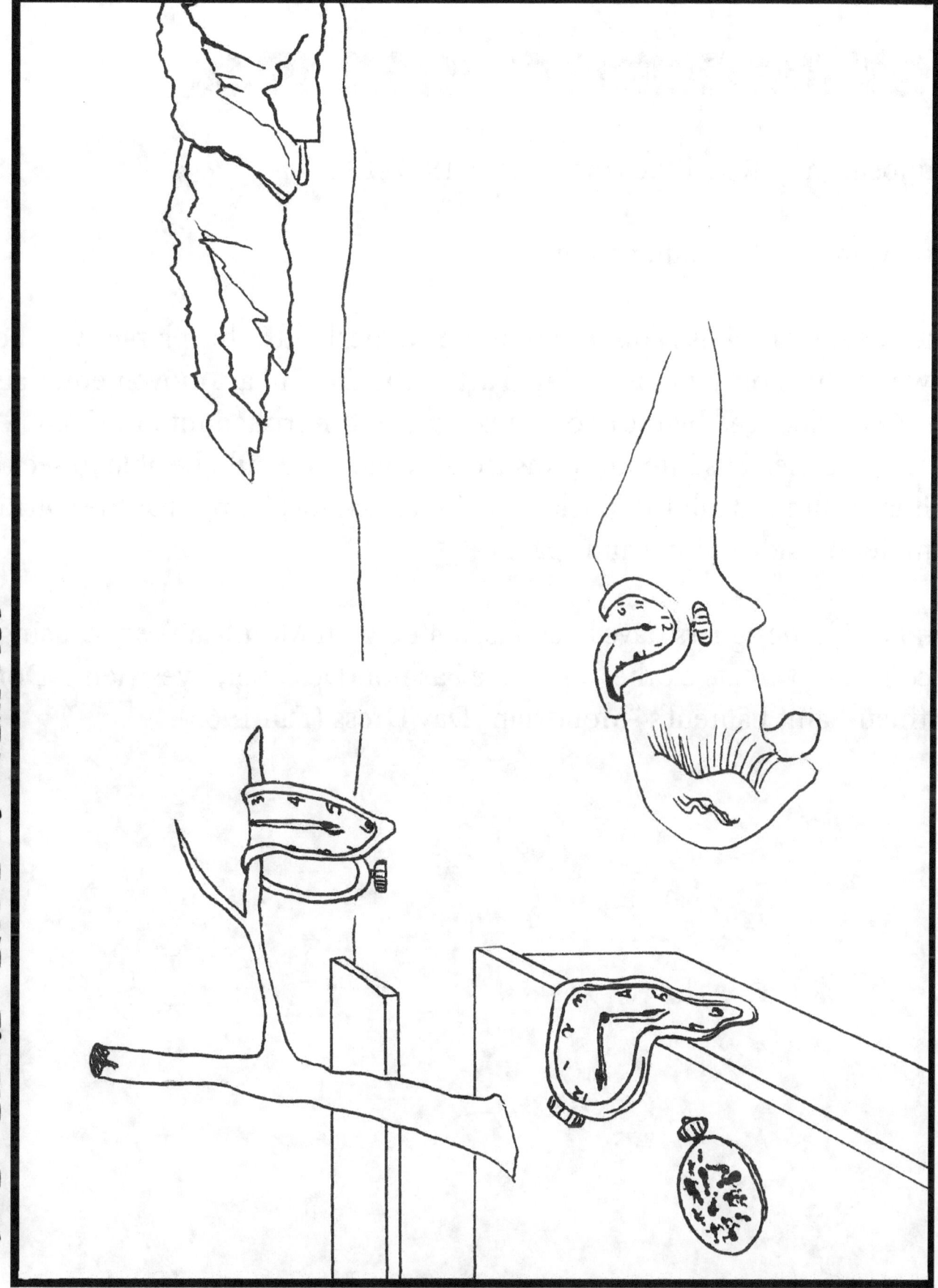

Piet Mondrian, 1872-1944

Composition in Red, Blue, and Yellow, 1937-1942

Oil on Canvas, Tate Gallery, London

Born Pieter Cornelius Mondriaan in the Netherlands, this painter was best known for his non-representational art in the De Stijl art movement. His style was influenced by Picasso and Braque but morphed into the Neo-Placticism style. His intention was that the viewer would be able to see the spiritual realm though his blocks of color and value, being that the spiritual realm lies outside of time and space.

Even fashion designers have been fascinated with Mondrian's style, using the concept to create clothes, as in the Fashion Designer, Yves Henri-Donat Matthieu-Saint Laurent's "Mondrian" Day Dress (Fall 1965).

COMPOSITION IN RED, BLUE, AND YELLOW

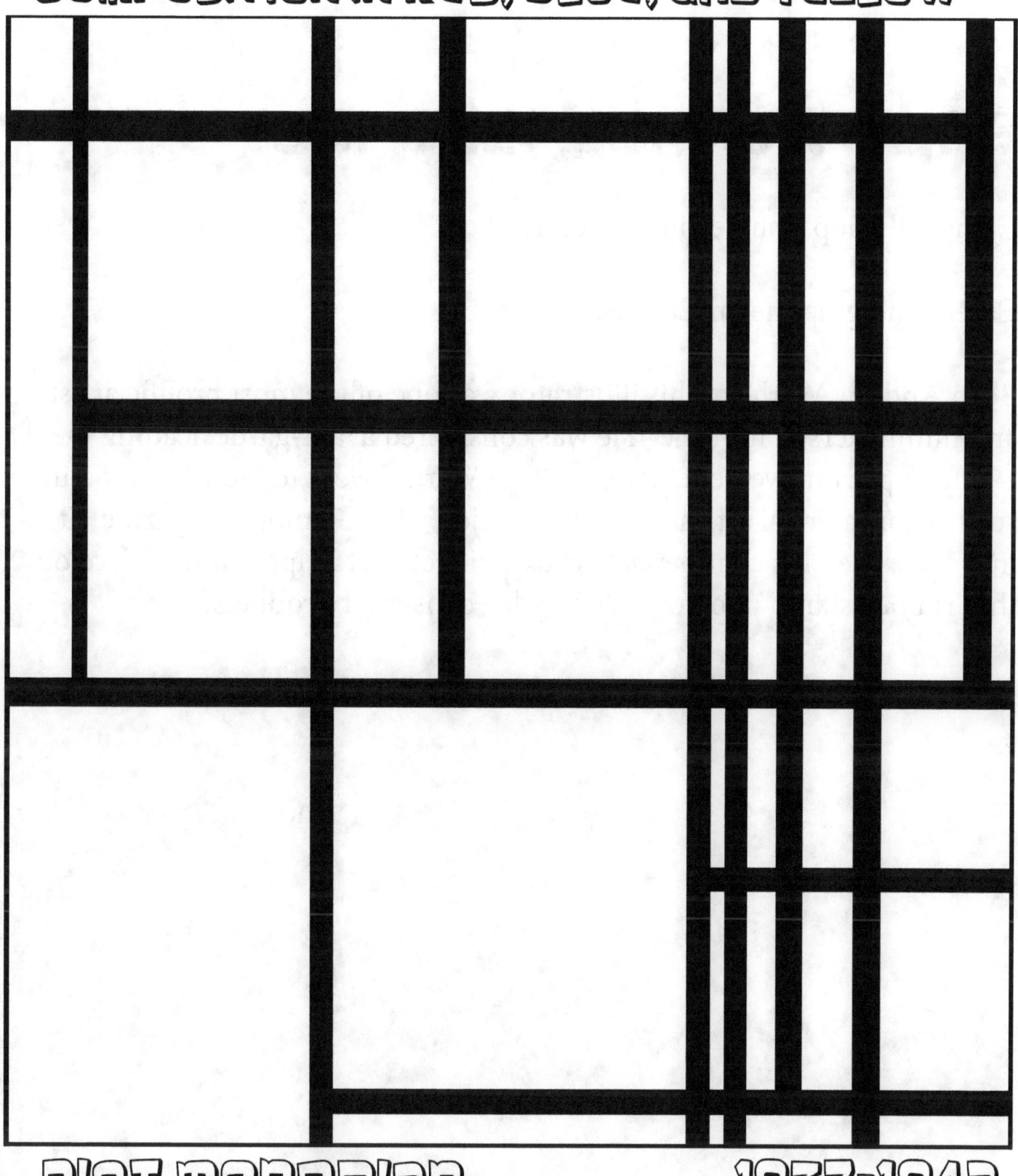

PIET MONDRIAN

1937-1942

anDY WaRHOL, 1928-1987

Campbell Soup Can Peeling Label, 1931

Casein and graphite on Canvas,

Born Andrew Warhola, this illustrator was one of the most prolific artists and filmmakers of his time. He was considered avant-garde, leading the 1960's Pop art movement. After college Warhol went to New York to pursue his commercial art career, landing a job with Glamour magazine. It may have been his commercial art experience that helped him to develop the "rubber-stamp" look of his everyday consumer products.

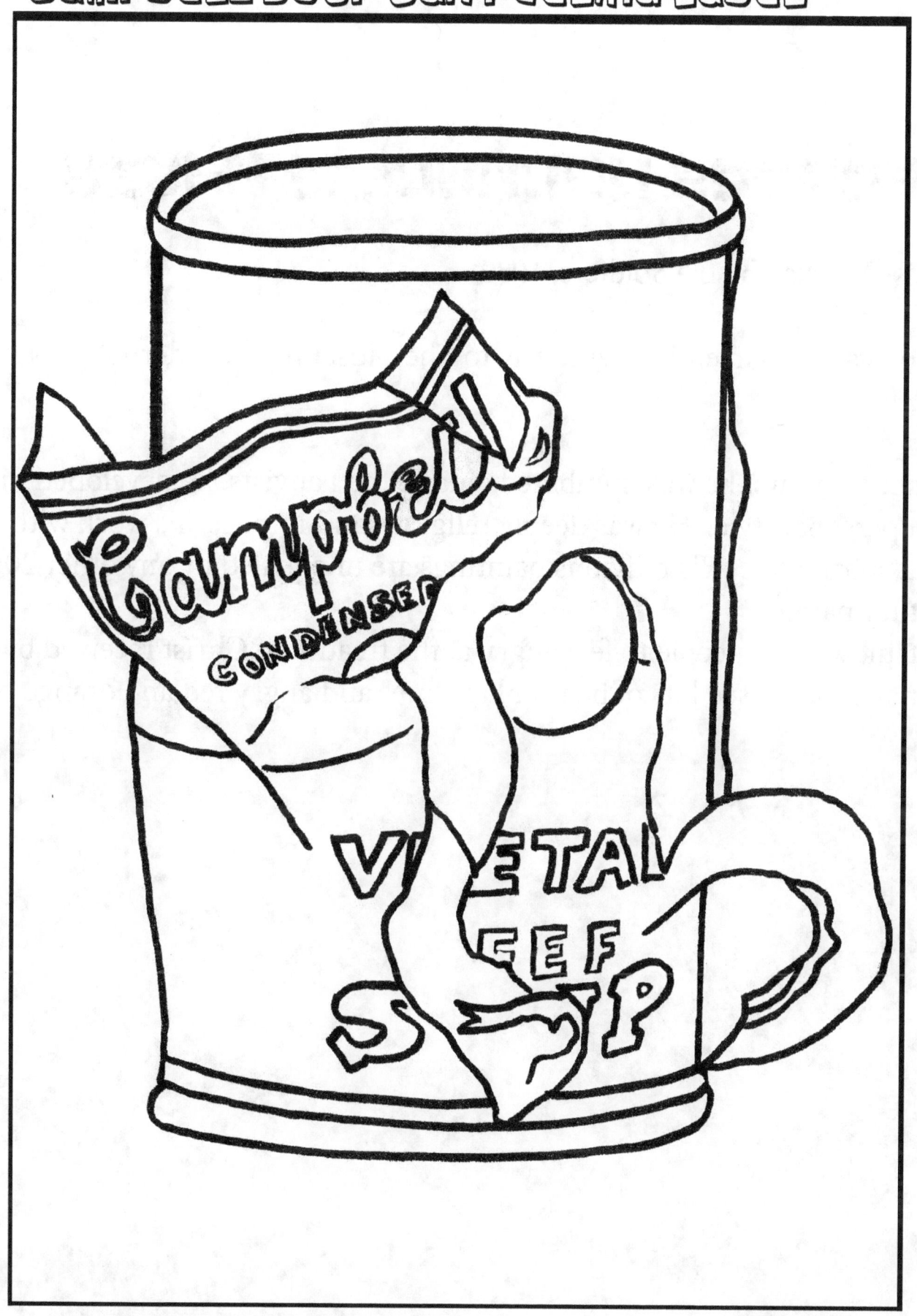

ANDY WARHOL   1931

GEORGES ROUAULT, 1871-1958

Christ Mocked by the Soldiers, 1932

Oil on canvas, Given anonymously to The Museum of Modern Art, New York

Although at first he was numbered among the Fauvists, he developed his own personal style. He was deeply religious and imbued his work with great spirituality. His religious paintings are unequaled by any other 20th century painter.

Rouault wanted people to feel angry at the treatment Christ received by the Romans so he used lots of heavy black lines and angry red and orange colors.

CHRIST MOCKED BY THE SOLDIERS

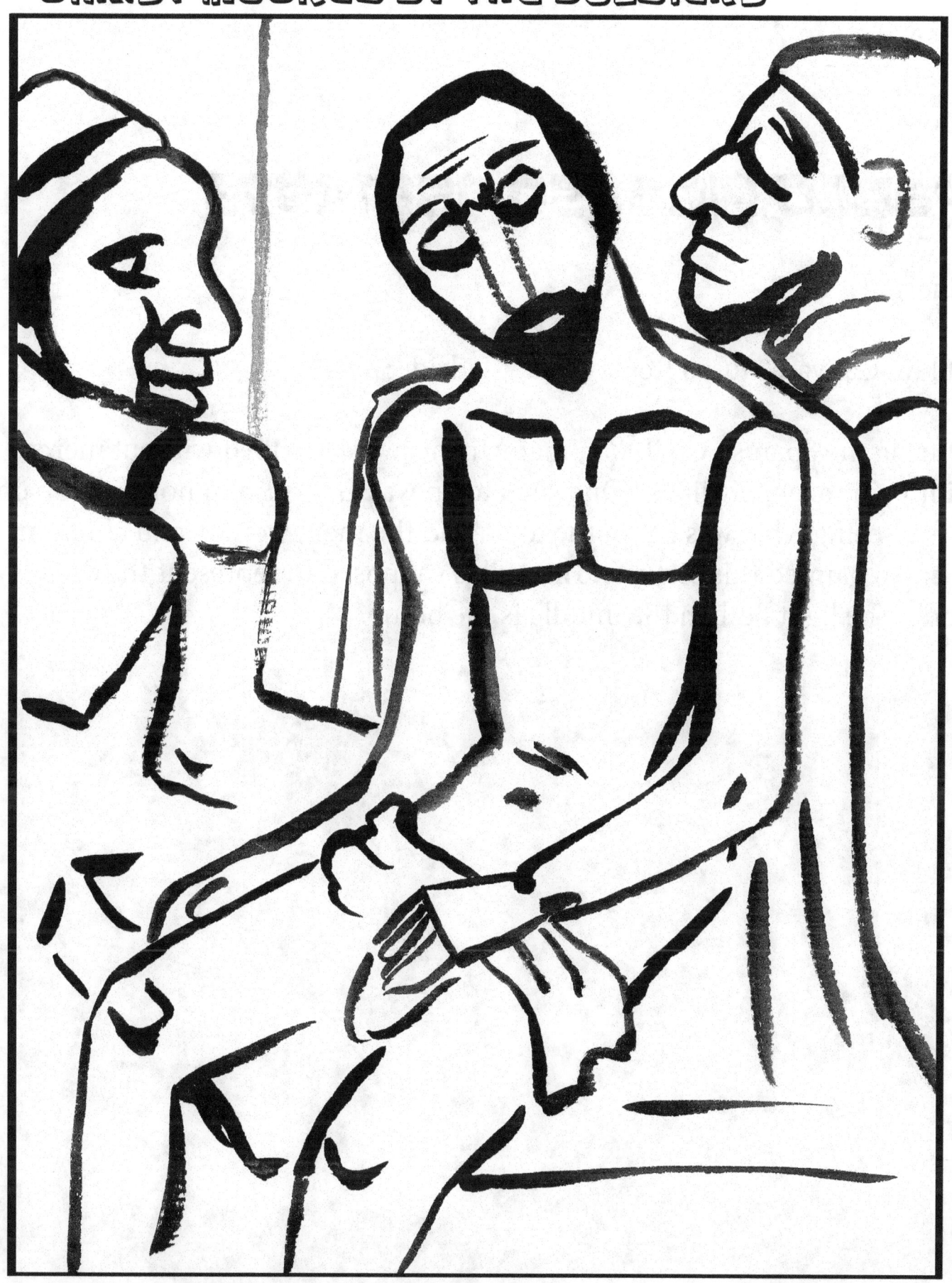

GEORGES ROUAULT   1932

Pablo Picasso, 1881-1973

Guernica, 1937

Oil on Canvas, Museo Reina Sofia, Madrid, Spain

During the Spanish Civil War, many towns were bombed without mercy killing innocent civilians. One such town was Guernica in northern Spain. After seeing what was left of the town and the men, women and children, Picasso painted this picture. The bull is supposed to represent the oppressors. The light bulb in the middle is the bomb.

GUERNICA

PABLO PICASSO

1937

MARC CHAGALL, 1887-1985

The Dance and The Circus, 1950

Oil on Canvas, Tate collection, Great Britain

Born Moishe Segal in Russia to a simple Jewish family, Chagall was banned from public schools for his faith. For many years he painted and studied in Saint Petersburg, relying on well-to-do friends to help his meager circumstances. When he was given a scholarship to study in Paris, he began using the pseudonym of Marc Chagall. He referred to his wife Bella as his love, his life, his muse. His style is considered modernist. During his lifetime, he created paintings, book illustrations, stained glass windows, and theatrical set designs, just to name a few.

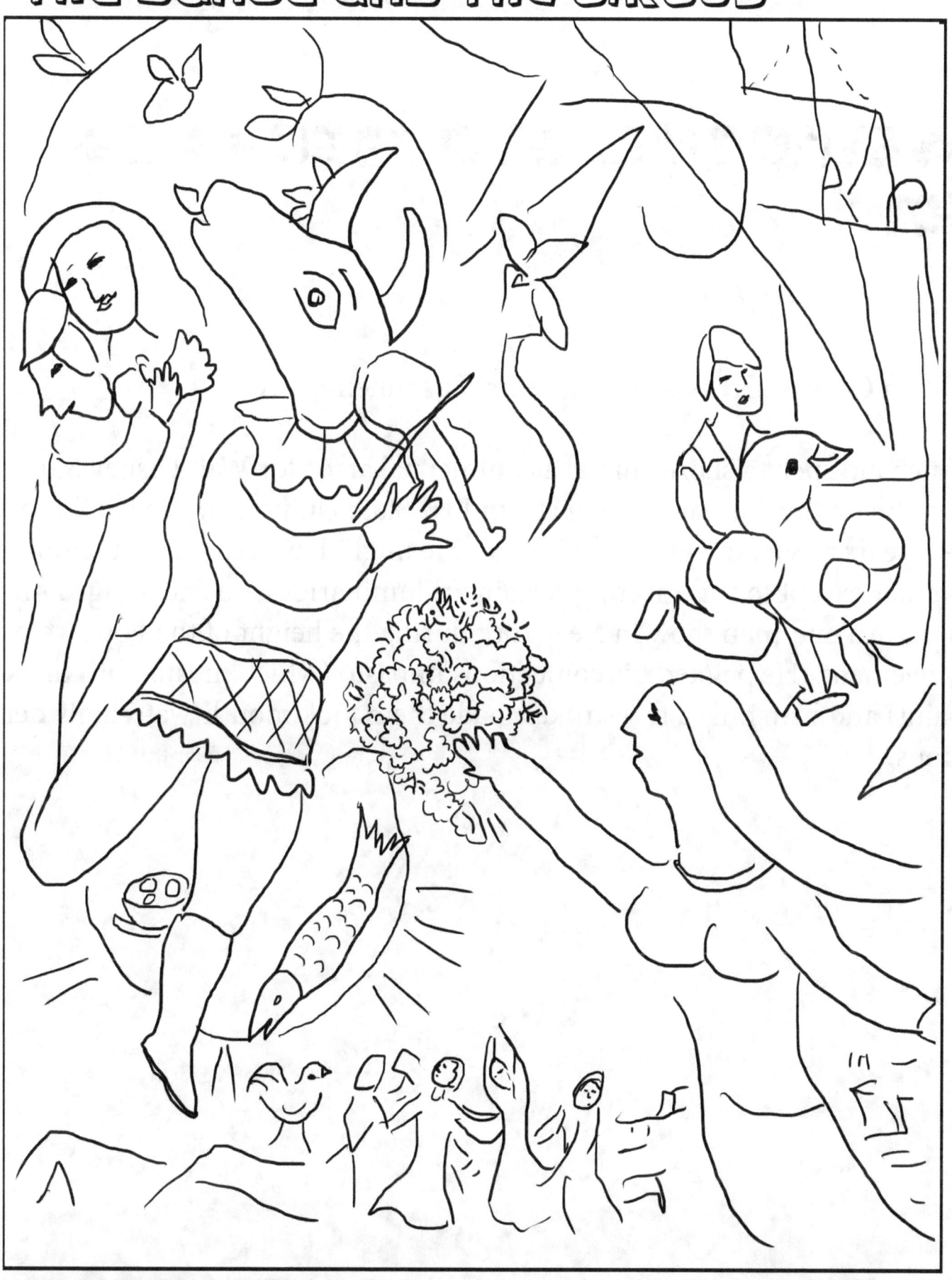

MARC CHIGALL   1950

wayne thiebaud, 1920-present

Pies, Pies, Pies, 1961

Oil on Canvas, Crocker Art Museum, Sacramento CA

Thiebaud spent a short time as a commercial artist for Walt Disney Studios before his formal training at San Jose State University. He taught for a few years at Sacramento City College. He might have remained a regional painter except for his meeting certain art luminaries who encouraged him to have a one-man show in New York during the height of the Pop Art Movement. He painted his confections impasto (which means with thick paint) and with only a few strokes made them look mouth-wateringly delicious.

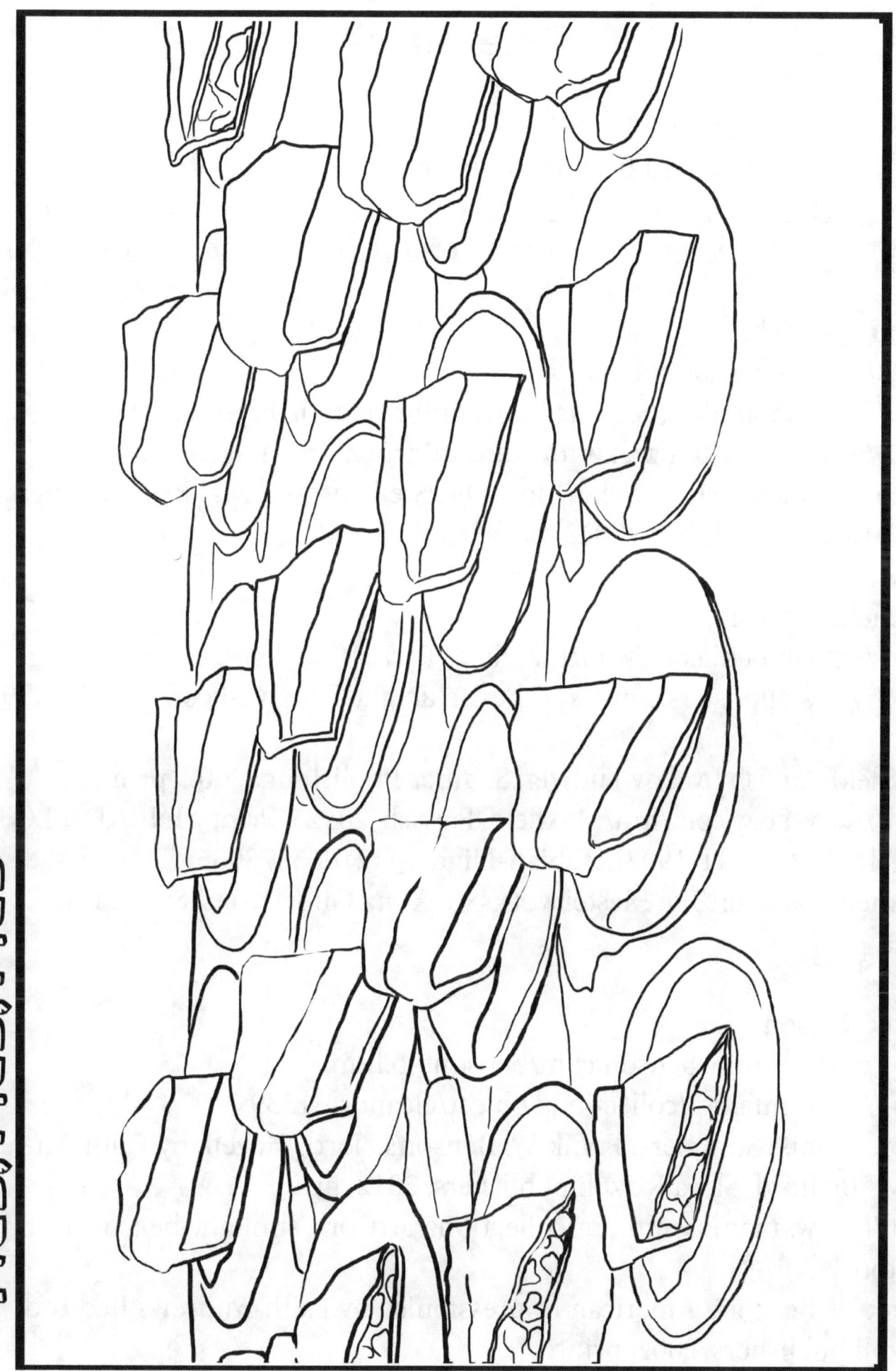

PIeS, PIeS, PIeS

WayNe THIeBauD

1961

References

After the Impressionists
Information referenced from the following sites:
http://arthistory.about.com/cs/reference/a/art_history_one_3.htm
http://arthistory.about.com/cs/reference/a/art_history_one_4.htm

Eduard Munch
http://www.edvardmunch.info/
http://www.edvardmunch.info/more-information/the-scream/
http://www.edvardmunch.info/more-information/the-scream/
Edvard Munch: 1863-1944, by Jon-Ove Steihaug and Mai Britt Guleng, Skira Rizzoli Publishers, 2013, print.

Maxfield Parrish
http://en.wikipedia.org/wiki/Maxfield_Parrish
http://www.allposters.com/-sp/The-Reluctant-Dragon-Posters_i2887419_.htm
Maxfield Parrish by Coy Ludwig, Schiffer Publishing, 2007, print.
http://www.ebay.com/itm/Maxfield-Parrish-20x25-Print-SINBAD-PLOTS-AGAINST-GIANT-1907-Arabian-Nights-/121065878006
Maxfield Parrish: The Masterworks by Alma Gilbert, Ten Speed Press, 2001, print.

Frank Benson
http://www.frankwbenson.com/bensonbio.html
http://www.mfa.org/collections/object/eleanor-31339
Impressionist Summers: Frank W. Benson's North Haven, by Faith Andrews Bedford, Skira Rizzoli publishers, 2012, print.
http://www.imamuseum.org/collections/artwork/sunlight-benson-frank-weston
Frank W. Benson: American Impressionist, by Faith Andrews Bedford, Rizzoli publishers, 2002, print.

Pablo Picasso
http://www.biography.com/people/pablo-picasso-9440021
http://www.wikipaintings.org/en/pablo-picasso/harlequin-leaning-1909
A Life of Picasso: The Prodigy, 1881-1906, by John Richardson, Knopf publishers, 2007, print.
http://en.wikipedia.org/wiki/Guernica_(painting)

John Singer Sargent
http://www.biography.com/people/john-singer-sargent-9471905
http://www.jssgallery.org/Paintings/Two_Girls_Fishing.htm
John Singer Sargent, by Carter Ratcliff, Abbeville Press, 2001, print.

Norman Rockwell
http://www.nrm.org/about-2/about-norman-rockwell/
http://bogus-boggess.blogspot.com/2007_12_01_archive.html
Norman Rockwell: A Life, by Laura Claridge, Modern Library publishers, 2003, print.

Georgia O'Keeffe
http://www.mfa.org/collections/object/white-rose-with-larkspur-no-2-34352
http://www.okeeffemuseum.org/
Georgia O'Keeffe and Her Houses: Ghost Ranch and Abiquiu by Barbara Buhler Lynes and Agapita Judy Lopez, Abrams Publishers, 2012, print.

Grant Wood
http://www.crma.org/content/grant_wood/Gallery.aspx
Grant Wood: A Life, by R. Tripp Evans, Knopf publishers, 2010, print.
http://en.wikipedia.org/wiki/American_Gothic
Artist in Overalls: The Life of Grant Wood, by John Buggleby, Chronicle Books, 1996, print.

Salvador Dali

http://en.wikipedia.org/wiki/The_Persistence_of_Memory

http://en.wikipedia.org/wiki/Salvador_Dal%C3%AD

Salvador Dali, The Paintings, by Robert Deschames and Giles Naret, Taschen publishers, 2013, print.

Pied Mondrian

http://www.biography.com/people/piet-mondrian-9411728

http://dressedinrococo.wordpress.com/2013/04/26/art-of-the-week-composition-ii-in-red-blue-and-yellow-by-piet-mondrian-1930/

Piet Mondrian: Life and Work, by Michel Seuphor, H.N. Abrams publishers, 1956, print.

Andy Warhol

http://www.biography.com/people/andy-warhol-9523875

Warhol: The Biography, by Victor Bockris, Da Capo Press, 2003, print.

Georges Rouault

http://www.moma.org/collection/provenance/provenance_object.php?object_id=79640

http://www.lesliesacks.com/artists/georges-rouault-1/bio

Georges Rouault: The Passion, by Timothy Mitchell, Dover Publishers, 1983, print.

Marc Chagall

http://www.marcchagallart.net/

http://www.tate.org.uk/art/artworks/chagall-the-dance-and-the-circus-n06135

Marc Chagall (Getting to Know the World's Greatest Artist), by Mike Venezia, Children's Press, 2000, print.

Wayne Thiebaud

http://en.wikipedia.org/wiki/Wayne_Thiebaud

http://crockerartmuseum.org/digital-crocker/item/pies-pies-pies-1961

Delicious: The Art and Life of Wayne Thiebaud, by Susan Goldman Rubin, Chronicle Books, 2007, print.

Bibliography

Art History, After the Impressionists, http://arthistory.about.com/cs/reference/a/art_history_one_3.htm

Art History, After Cubists and Fauves, http://arthistory.about.com/cs/reference/a/art_history_one_4.htm

Munch, Edvard, biography, http://www.edvardmunch.info/

Munch, Edvard, The Scream, painting, http://www.edvardmunch.info/more-information/the-scream/

Edvard Munch: 1863-1944, by Jon-Ove Steihaug and Mai Britt Guleng, Skira Rizzoli Publishers, 2013, print.

http://www.moma.org/collection/provenance/provenance_object.php?object_id=79640
http://www.lesliesacks.com/artists/georges-rouault-1/bio

www.ingramcontent.com/pod-product-compliance
Lightning Source LLC
Chambersburg PA
CBHW081624170526
45166CB00009B/3093

* 9 7 8 1 5 0 0 5 8 5 2 2 8 *